by Iain Gray

Lang**Syne**
PUBLISHING
WRITING *to* REMEMBER

E-mail: info@lang-syne.co.uk

Distributed in the Republic of Ireland by Portfolio Group,
Kilbarrack Ind. Est. Kilbarrack, Dublin 5.
T:00353(01) 839 4918 F:00353(01) 839 5826
sales@portfoliogroup.ie
www.portfoliogroup.ie

Design by Dorothy Meikle   Printed by Ricoh Print Scotland

ISBN 978-1-85217-250-3

Doyle

MOTTO:
He conquers by fortitude.

CREST:
A buck's head attired with a ducal coronet.

NAME variations include:

Ó Dubhghaill *(Gaelic)*	MacDowell
Ó Dúill *(Gaelic)*	McDougal
O'Doyle	McDougall
Doyel	McDoughall
Dougall	McDowall
Dowell	McDowel
MacDowall	McDowell

Chapter one:
Origins of Irish surnames

According to an old saying, there are two types of Irish – those who actually are Irish and those who wish they were.

This sentiment is only one example of the allure that the high romance and drama of the proud nation's history holds for thousands of people scattered across the world today.

It's a sad fact, however, that the vast majority of Irish surnames are found far beyond Irish shores, rather than on the Emerald Isle itself.

The population stood at around eight million souls in 1841, but today it stands at fewer than six million.

This is mainly a tragic consequence of the potato famine, also known as the Great Hunger, which devastated Ireland between 1845 and 1849.

The Irish peasantry had become almost wholly reliant for basic sustenance on the potato, first introduced from the Americas in the seventeenth century.

When the crop was hit by a blight, at least 800,000 people starved to death while an estimated two million others were forced to seek a new life far from their native shores – particularly in America, Canada, and Australia.

The effects of the potato blight continued until about 1851, by which time a firm pattern of emigration had become established.

Ireland's loss, however, was to the gain of the countries in which the immigrants settled, contributing enormously, as their descendants do today, to the well being of the nations in which their forefathers settled.

But those who were forced through dire circumstance to establish a new life in foreign parts never forgot their roots, or the proud heritage and traditions of the land that gave them birth.

Nor do their descendants.

It is a heritage that is inextricably bound up in the colourful variety of Irish names themselves – and the origin and history of these names forms an integral part of the vibrant drama that is the nation's history, one of both glorious fortune and tragic misfortune.

This history is well documented, and one of the most important and fascinating of the earliest sources are *The Annals of the Four Masters*, compiled between 1632 and 1636 by four friars at the Franciscan Monastery in County Donegal.

Compiled from earlier sources, and purporting to go back to the Biblical Deluge, much of the material takes in the mythological origins and history of Ireland and the Irish.

This includes tales of successive waves of invaders and settlers such as the Fomorians, the Partholonians, the Nemedians, the Fir Bolgs, the Tuatha De Danann, and the Laigain.

Of particular interest are the *Milesian Genealogies*,

because the majority of Irish clans today claim a descent from either Heremon, Ir, or Heber – three of the sons of Milesius, a king of what is now modern day Spain.

These sons invaded Ireland in the second millennium B.C, apparently in fulfilment of a mysterious prophecy received by their father.

This Milesian lineage is said to have ruled Ireland for nearly 3,000 years, until the island came under the sway of England's King Henry II in 1171 following what is known as the Cambro-Norman invasion.

This is an important date not only in Irish history in general, but for the effect the invasion subsequently had for Irish surnames.

'Cambro' comes from the Welsh, and 'Cambro-Norman' describes those Welsh knights of Norman origin who invaded Ireland.

But they were invaders who stayed, inter-marrying with the native Irish population and founding their own proud dynasties that bore Cambro-Norman names such as Archer, Barbour, Brannagh, Fitzgerald, Fitzgibbon, Fleming, Joyce, Plunkett, and Walsh – to name only a few.

These 'Cambro-Norman' surnames that still flourish throughout the world today form one of the three main categories in which Irish names can be placed – those of Gaelic-Irish, Cambro-Norman, and Anglo-Irish.

Previous to the Cambro-Norman invasion of the twelfth century, and throughout the earlier invasions and settlement of those wild bands of sea rovers known as the Vikings in the eighth and ninth centuries, the population of the island was relatively small, and it was normal for a person to be identified through the use of only a forename.

But as population gradually increased and there were many more people with the same forename, surnames were adopted to distinguish one person, or one community, from another.

Individuals identified themselves with their own particular tribe, or 'tuath', and this tribe – that also became known as a clann, or clan – took its name from some distinguished ancestor who had founded the clan.

The Gaelic-Irish form of the name Kelly, for example, is Ó Ceallaigh, or O'Kelly, indicating descent from an original 'Ceallaigh', with the 'O' denoting 'grandson of.' The name was later anglicised to Kelly.

The prefix 'Mac' or 'Mc', meanwhile, as with the clans of the Scottish Highlands, denotes 'son of.'

Although the Irish clans had much in common with their Scottish counterparts, one important difference lies in what are known as 'septs', or branches, of the clan.

Septs of Scottish clans were groups who often bore an entirely different name from the clan name but were under the clan's protection.

In Ireland, septs were groups that shared the same name and who could be found scattered throughout the four provinces of Ulster, Leinster, Munster, and Connacht.

The 'golden age' of the Gaelic-Irish clans, infused as their veins were with the blood of Celts, pre-dates the Viking invasions of the eighth and ninth centuries and the Norman invasion of the twelfth century, and the sacred heart of the country was the Hill of Tara, near the River Boyne, in County Meath.

Known in Gaelic as 'Teamhar na Rí', or Hill of Kings, it was the royal seat of the 'Ard Rí Éireann', or High King of Ireland, to whom the petty kings, or chieftains, from the island's provinces were ultimately subordinate.

It was on the Hill of Tara, beside a stone pillar known as the Irish 'Lia Fáil', or Stone of Destiny, that the High Kings were inaugurated and, according to legend, this stone would emit a piercing screech that could be heard all over Ireland when touched by the hand of the rightful king.

The Hill of Tara is today one of the island's main tourist attractions.

Opposition to English rule over Ireland, established in the wake of the Cambro-Norman invasion, broke out frequently and the harsh solution adopted by the powerful forces of the Crown was to forcibly evict the native Irish from their lands.

These lands were then granted to Protestant colonists, or 'planters', from Britain.

Many of these colonists, ironically, came from Scotland and were the descendants of the original 'Scotti', or 'Scots', who gave their name to Scotland after migrating there in the fifth century A.D., from the north of Ireland.

Colonisation entailed harsh penal laws being imposed on the majority of the native Irish population, stripping them practically of all of their rights.

The Crown's main bastion in Ireland was Dublin and its environs, known as the Pale, and it was the dispossessed peasantry who lived outside this Pale, desperately striving to eke out a meagre living.

It was this that gave rise to the modern-day expression of someone or something being 'beyond the pale'.

Attempts were made to stamp out all aspects of the ancient Gaelic-Irish culture, to the extent that even to bear a Gaelic-Irish name was to invite discrimination.

This is why many Gaelic-Irish names were anglicised with, for example, and noted above, Ó Ceallaigh, or O'Kelly, being anglicised to Kelly.

Succeeding centuries have seen strong revivals of Gaelic-Irish consciousness, however, and this has led to many families reverting back to the original form of their name, while the language itself is frequently found on the fluent tongues of an estimated 90,000 to 145,000 of the island's population.

Ireland's turbulent history of religious and political strife is one that lasted well into the twentieth century, a landmark century that saw the partition of the island into the twenty-six counties of the independent Republic of

Ireland, or Eire, and the six counties of Northern Ireland, or
Ulster.

Dublin, originally founded by Vikings, is now a vibrant
and truly cosmopolitan city while the proud city of Belfast
is one of the jewels in the crown of Ulster.

It was Saint Patrick who first brought the light of
Christianity to Ireland in the fifth century A.D.

Interpretations of this Christian message have varied
over the centuries, often leading to bitter sectarian conflict –
but the many intricately sculpted Celtic Crosses found all
over the island are symbolic of a unity that crosses the
sectarian divide.

It is an image that fuses the 'old gods' of the Celts with
Christianity.

All the signs from the early years of this new
millennium indicate that sectarian strife may soon become a
thing of the past – with the Irish and their many kinsfolk
across the world, be they Protestant or Catholic, finding
common purpose in the rich tapestry of their shared
heritage.

Chapter two:

The dark foreigners

One clue to the ancient roots of the proud clan of Doyle can be found in the original Gaelic form of the name, 'Ó Dubhghaill'.

The name indicates 'dark foreigner', with 'dubh' signifying dark, or black, and 'ghaill', or 'gall', indicating foreigner.

It was indeed as 'dark foreigners' that the ancestors of the Doyles of today first arrived on the Emerald Isle, but this was at a period so far back through the dim mists of time that they eventually became as proudly 'native Irish' as the native Irish they first encountered.

They certainly did not come bearing gifts, but fire and sword, as they pillaged the island from end to end leaving a trail of devastation in their wake.

For these ancestors of the Doyles were the fierce Scandinavian sea rovers more commonly known as Vikings.

Mainly of Norwegian origin, it was in the closing years of the eighth century A.D. that their sinister longboats first appeared off Irish shores, and the monastery of St. Patrick's Island, near Skerries in present day Co. Dublin was looted and burned to the ground.

Raids continued along the coastline until they made

their first forays inland in 836 A.D., while a year later a Viking fleet of 60 vessels sailed into the River Boyne.

An indication of the terror they brought can be found in one contemporary account of their depredations and desecrations.

It lamented how 'the pagans desecrated the sanctuaries of God, and poured out the blood of saints upon the altar, laid waste the house of our hope, trampled on the bodies of saints in the temple of God, like dung in the street.'

By 841 A.D. the Vikings, or Ostmen as they were also known, had established a number of strongholds on the island, but their raids began to ease off before returning with a terrifying and bloody vengeance in about 914 A.D.

They met with a determined resistance from the native Irish, most notably in the form of the forces of the powerful confederation of clans known as the southern Uí Neill.

The Irish suffered a resounding defeat at the battle of Dublin in 919 A.D., and it was not until just over thirty years later that the raids gradually came to an end.

By this time the Viking ancestors of the Doyles of today had established permanent settlements in Ireland, part-icularly in Dublin and other coastal areas such as present day Waterford, Wexford, Carlingford, and Strangford – indeed the names of the latter four stem from the Old Norse language of the Scandinavians.

Interestingly the present day county of Wexford is where many Doyles of today can be found.

Having put aside the broadsword and battleaxe in favour of the more peaceful pursuit of trade, the Ostmen contributed significantly to Ireland's fortunes by, for example, establishing Dublin as a main European trading port.

By the late tenth and early eleventh centuries Ireland was the scene of vicious inter-clan rivalry as successive clan chiefs fought for supremacy over their rivals.

By 1002 A.D. Brian Boruma, better known to posterity as Brian Boru, had achieved the prize of the High Kingship of Ireland – but there were still rival chieftains, and not least the Ostmen, to deal with.

Resenting Brian Boru's High Kingship, a number of chieftains, particularly those of the province of Leinster, found common cause with the Ostmen, and the two sides met in final and bloody confrontation at the battle of Clontarf, about four miles north of Dublin, on Good Friday, 1014.

Boru proved victorious, but the annals speak of great slaughter on the day, with the dead piled high on the field of battle, including three of his sons.

The king had little time to celebrate his victory – being killed in his tent by a party of fleeing Vikings, but not before felling most of them with his great two-handed sword.

'Ó Dubhghaill' had been the nickname given by the Irish to those 'dark foreigners' who had first arrived on the island with fire and sword, but those who chose to settle on the island rapidly assimilated the Irish way of life.

'Ó Dubhghaills', or Doyles as they would become, were also to be found in later centuries in the form of the name of MacDughaill, or MacDowell.

These 'Doyles' had first come to Ireland from the Western Isles of Scotland in about the middle of the thirteenth century as 'galloglasses', or mercenary soldiers, in the service of clans such as the O' Connors.

Originally settled in the area of present day Co. Roscommon, they later settled in Ulster and, in common with their 'Doyle' counterparts who had first arrived in Ireland centuries before, they were of Scandinavian stock.

Whatever their origins, the Irish clans found common cause in the late twelfth century and the centuries following in resisting yet another powerful invader.

Twelfth century Ireland was far from being a unified nation, split up as it was into territories ruled over by ambitious chieftains who ruled as kings in their own right.

In a series of bloody conflicts one chieftain, or king, would occasionally gain the upper hand over his rivals, and by 1156 the most powerful was Muirchertach MacLochlainn, king of the powerful O'Neills.

The equally powerful Rory O'Connor, king of the province of Connacht, opposed him but he increased his power and influence by allying himself with Dermot MacMurrough, king of Leinster.

MacLochlainn and MacMurrough were aware that the main key to the kingdom of Ireland was the thriving trading port of Dublin that had been established by the Ostmen.

Dublin was taken by the combined forces of the Leinster and Connacht kings, but when MacLochlainn died the Dubliners rose up in revolt and overthrew the unpopular MacMurrough.

A triumphant Rory O'Connor entered Dublin and was later inaugurated as Ard Rí, but the proud Dermott MacMurrough refused to accept defeat.

He appealed for help from England's Henry II in unseating O'Connor – an act that was to radically affect the future course of Ireland's fortunes in general and those of clans such as the Doyles in particular.

Chapter three:

Conquest and rebellion

The English monarch, who had already had his own avaricious eyes on Ireland, agreed to help MacMurrough, but distanced himself from direct action by delegating his Norman subjects in Wales with the task.

These ambitious and battle-hardened barons and knights had first settled in Wales following the Norman Conquest of England in 1066 and, with an eye on rich booty, plunder, and lands, were only too eager to obey their sovereign's wishes and furnish MacMurrough with aid.

MacMurrough crossed the Irish Sea to Bristol, where he rallied powerful barons such as Robert Fitzstephen and Maurice Fitzgerald to his cause, along with Gilbert de Clare, Earl of Pembroke.

The mighty Norman war machine soon moved into action, and so fierce and disciplined was their onslaught on the forces of Rory O'Connor and his allies that by 1171 they had re-captured Dublin, in the name of MacMurrough, and other strategically important territories.

Henry II began to take cold feet over the venture, realising that he may have created a rival in the form of a separate Norman kingdom in Ireland.

Accordingly, he landed on the island, near Waterford, at

the head of a large army in October of 1171 with the aim of curbing the power of his Cambro-Norman barons.

Protracted war between the king and his barons was averted, however, when they submitted to the royal will, promising homage and allegiance in return for holding the territories they had conquered in the king's name.

Henry also received the submission and homage of many of the Irish chieftains, tired as they were with internecine warfare and also perhaps realising that as long as they were rivals and not united they were no match for the powerful forces the English Crown could muster.

English dominion over Ireland was ratified through the Treaty of Windsor of 1175, under the terms of which Rory O'Connor, for example, was allowed to rule territory unoccupied by the Normans in the role of a vassal of the king.

Over succeeding centuries the Crown's grip on the island intensified to the extent that three separate Irelands were created.

These were the territories of the privileged and powerful Anglo-Norman barons and their retainers, the Ireland of the disaffected Gaelic-Irish who held lands unoccupied by the original invaders and the Pale – comprised of Dublin itself and a substantial area of its environs ruled over by an English elite.

It was a recipe for frequent rebellion, one of the bloodiest of which erupted in 1641 in the form of a rebellion by Catholic landowners such as the Doyles against the English Crown's policy of settling, or 'planting' loyal Protestants on Irish land.

This policy had started during the reign from 1491 to 1547 of Henry VIII, whose Reformation effectively outlawed the established Roman Catholic faith throughout his dominions.

This settlement of loyal Protestants in Ireland continued throughout the subsequent reigns of Elizabeth I, James I (James VI of Scotland), and Charles I.

In the insurrection that exploded in 1641, at least 2,000 Protestant settlers were massacred at the hands of Catholic landowners and their native Irish peasantry, while thousands more were stripped of their belongings and driven from their lands.

Terrible as the atrocities were against the Protestant settlers, subsequent accounts became greatly exaggerated, serving to fuel a burning desire on the part of Protestants for revenge against the rebels.

Tragically for Ireland, this revenge became directed not only against the rebels, but Irish Catholics such as the Doyles in general.

The English Civil War intervened to prevent immediate action against the rebels, but following the execution of Charles I in 1649 and the consolidation of the power of the English Protestant, Oliver Cromwell, the time was ripe for revenge.

The Lord Protector, as he was named, descended on Ireland at the head of a 20,000-strong army that landed at Ringford, near Dublin, in August of 1649.

The consequences of this Cromwellian conquest still resonate throughout the island today.

Cromwell had three main aims: to quash all forms of rebellion, to 'remove' all Catholic landowners who had taken part in the rebellion, and to convert the native Irish to the Protestant faith.

An early warning of the terrors that were in store for the native Catholic Irish came when the northeastern town of Drogheda was stormed and taken in September and between 2,000 and 4,000 of its inhabitants killed, including priests who were summarily put to the sword.

Sir Arthur Aston, who had refused to surrender the town, was captured and brutally clubbed to death with his wooden leg – the blood-crazed Cromwellian troopers having mistakenly believed he had stuffed it with gold pieces.

The defenders of Drogheda's St. Peter's Church, who had also refused to surrender, were burned to death as they huddled for refuge in the steeple and the church was deliberately torched.

A similar fate awaited Wexford, on the southeast coast, and a main base of the Doyles.

At least 1,500 of its inhabitants were slaughtered, including 200 defenceless women, despite their pathetic pleas for mercy.

Three hundred other inhabitants of the town drowned when their overladen boats sank as they desperately tried to flee to safety, while a group of Franciscan friars were massacred in their church – some as they knelt before the altar.

The Wexford massacre is commemorated today in the form of a statue and plaque at the town's Bull Ring.

Cromwell soon held Ireland in a grip of iron, allowing him to implement what amounted to a policy of ethnic cleansing.

His troopers were given free rein to hunt down and kill priests, while Catholic estates, such as Doyle estates in Wexford, were confiscated.

Catholic landowners in Ulster, Leinster, and Munster were grudgingly given pathetically small estates west of the river Shannon – where they were hemmed in by colonies of Cromwellian soldiers.

Following the devastations that came in the wake of the Cromwellian invasion, the final death knell of the ancient Gaelic order of proud Irish clans such as the Doyles was sounded.

This was in the form of what is known in Ireland as Cogadh an Dá Rí, or The War of the Two Kings.

Also known as the Williamite War in Ireland or the Jacobite War in Ireland, it was sparked off in 1688 when the Stuart monarch James II (James VII of Scotland) was deposed and fled into exile in France.

The Protestant William of Orange and his wife Mary were invited to take up the thrones of Scotland, Ireland, and England – but James still had significant support in Ireland.

His supporters were known as Jacobites, and among them were several Doyles.

Following the arrival in England of William and Mary from Holland, Richard Talbot, 1st Earl of Tyrconnell and James's Lord Deputy in Ireland, assembled an army loyal to the Stuart cause.

The aim was to garrison and fortify the island in the name of James and quell any resistance.

Londonderry, or Derry, proved loyal to the cause of William of Orange, or William III as he had become, and managed to hold out against a siege that was not lifted until July 28, 1689.

James, with the support of troops and money supplied by Louis XIV of France, had landed at Kinsale in March of 1689 and joined forces with his Irish supporters.

A series of military encounters followed, culminating in James's defeat by an army commanded by William at the battle of the Boyne on July 12, 1689.

James fled again into French exile, never to return, while another significant Jacobite defeat occurred in July of 1691 at the battle of Aughrim – with about half their army killed on the field, wounded, or taken prisoner.

The Williamite forces besieged Limerick and the Jacobites were forced into surrender in September of 1691.

A peace treaty known as the Treaty of Limerick followed, under which those Jacobites willing to swear an oath of loyalty to William were allowed to remain in their native land.

Those reluctant to do so were allowed to seek exile on foreign shores – but their ancient homelands were lost to them forever.

It was at this stage that some Doyles, but by no means all, and in common with other Catholic families, converted to the Protestant faith in a desperate bid to retain what lands and privileges remained.

A further flight overseas occurred following an abortive rebellion in 1798, while Doyles were among the many thousands of Irish who were forced to seek a new life many thousands of miles from their native land during the famine known as The Great Hunger, caused by a failure of the potato crop between 1845 and 1849.

But in many cases Ireland's loss of sons and daughters such as the Doyles was to the gain of those equally proud nations in which they settled.

Chapter four:
On the world stage

Bearers of the proud name of Doyle have excelled, and continue to excel, in a wide range of pursuits that include art and literature, music, film and sport.

One of the most famous families of the name of Doyle is the one that includes the artist and political cartoonist **John Doyle**, who was born in Dublin in 1797 and died in 1868.

After studying art in his native city he moved to London, and it was here that he became famous as the *Punch Magazine* political cartoonist known as 'HB'.

His son **Richard Doyle**, born in 1824 and who died in 1883, also contributed to the magazine as a cartoonist, while his other son, **Charles Altamont-Doyle**, born in 1832 and who died in 1893, was the talented illustrator who was also the father of the great writer **Sir Arthur Conan Doyle**.

Born in Edinburgh in 1859, Conan Doyle was not only a short story writer and novelist but also a poet and a medical doctor.

After studying medicine at Edinburgh University from between 1876 to 1881 he worked for a time as a general practitioner in the English city of Birmingham.

There then followed a short period as a ship's doctor before he settled into medical practice in Plymouth in 1882.

Five years later, in 1887, the literary world was first introduced to the famous character of crime sleuth Sherlock Holmes in Doyle's novel *A Study in Scarlet*.

Many other celebrated tales of Sherlock Holmes followed this.

By the time of his death in 1930 Conan Doyle had been knighted and become the acclaimed author of a vast range of works of crime fiction, science fiction, plays, romances, poems, and non-fiction.

There is a statue of him in the East Sussex town of Crowborough, where he lived for a number of years, and also a statue of his literary character Sherlock Holmes in Picardy Place, in Conan Doyle's native Edinburgh.

His youngest son, **Adrian Conan Doyle**, born in Crowborough in 1910 and who died in 1970, became not only his father's literary executor but also an explorer, big-game hunter, race car driver, and writer.

The founder of the Arthur Conan Doyle Literary Foundation he also, with the collaboration of John Dickson Carr, published a number of Sherlock Holmes tales in the early 1950s based on characters and plots from his father's earlier stories.

These included *The Adventure of the Abbas Ruby*, sourced from the famous Arthur Conan Doyle story *The Hound of the Baskervilles*.

Born in 1912, Arthur Conan Doyle's daughter **Jean Conan Doyle** served for thirty years with Britain's

Women's Royal Air Force, attaining the rank of Air Commandant, in addition to serving as a time as an honorary Aide-de-Camp to Queen Elizabeth II.

She became Lady Bromet following her marriage to Air Vice-Marshall Sir Geoffrey Rhodes Bromet. She died in 1997.

In the world of acting **Tony Doyle**, born in 1942, was the Irish film and television actor who, in addition to winning an Irish Film and Television Academy Award for his role in the 1988 television series *Amongst Women*, also starred in television shows such as the popular *Ballykissangel*.

This was a series in which his daughter, the actress **Susannah Doyle**, born in 1966, starred after her father's death in 2000. She is also known for her roles in the British television comedy series *Drop The Dead Donkey* and the police drama *A Touch of Frost*.

Also on the stage Maria Doyle, known as **Maria Doyle Kennedy** following her marriage in 1992, is the Irish actress born in 1964 who sang for a time with the band Hothouse Flowers and has appeared in Irish-based films such as *The General* and *The Commitments*.

Born in 1929 in Omaha, Nebraska, **David Doyle** was the American actor best known for his role as John Bosley in the internationally popular television series *Charlie's Angels*. He died in 1997.

Born in 1956 in Brooklyn, New York, **Jerry Doyle** is

the actor and radio personality best known to international audiences for his role as Michael Garibaldi in the science fiction television series *Babylon 5*.

Behind the camera lens **Christopher Doyle**, born in 1952 in Sydney, is the Australian cinematographer whose many film credits include the 2005 *The White Countess* and the 2006 *Invisible Waves*.

He has also been behind acclaimed music videos for bands such as The Strokes and Texas.

Born in Dublin in 1970, **Craig Doyle** is a popular Irish radio and television presenter.

Doyles have also excelled in the world of music – and no less so than the Scottish musician and film screen composer **Patrick Doyle**, who was born in 1953 in Uddingston, South Lanarkshire.

Composer of orchestral scores for movies that include *Carlito's Way*, the 2001 *Bridget Jones' Diary*, *Gosford Park*, and *Harry Potter and the Goblet of Fire*, he also won a Golden Globe nomination and a BAFTA nomination in addition to an Oscar for Best Original Dramatic Score for his work on the 1995 *Sense and Sensibility*.

Born in 1969 in Petty Harbour, Newfoundland, **Alan Doyle** is a musician with the Canadian Celtic band Great Big Sea, while fellow Canadian **Damhnait Dolye**, born in 1975 in Labrador City, is the singer and guitarist who is a member of the group Shaye, in addition to being a successful solo performer.

Born in Belfast in 1963, **Candida Doyle** is the keyboard instrumentalist and occasional vocalist with the pop band Pulp.

In the world of the printed word **Roddy Doyle**, born in 1958 in Kilbarrack, Dublin is an accomplished Irish novelist and screenwriter.

Many of his works have been adapted for the screen, including the 1991 *The Commitments*, while his many awards include the Booker Prize in 1993 for his novel *Paddy Clarke Ha Ha*.

In the newspaper world **Richard Doyle**, who was better known as 'Doc', was the Canadian journalist, editor and Senator who was born in Toronto in 1923 and died in 2003.

An editor and later an editor-in-chief of the *Globe and Mail* newspaper, he was made a member of the Canadian News Hall of Fame in 1990, while he was also an officer of the Order of Canada.

Author of the best-selling memoir *A Great Feast of Light: Growing Up Irish in the Television Age*, **John Doyle** is the television critic for the *Globe and Mail* who was born in 1957 in Co. Tipperary.

He emigrated from his native Ireland to Canada in the 1980s and, apart from his work as a television critic, he also covers football events for the newspaper.

Doyles have also been, and continue to be, prominent in the highly competitive world of sport.

Born in 1948 in Woonsocket, Rhode Island, **Allen**

Doyle is the American golfer whose major wins at the time of writing include the 1999 Senior PGA Championship and the U.S. Senior Open in both 2005 and 2006.

On the athletics track **Simon Doyle**, born in 1966 in Queensland, is the former Australian runner who in 1991 set Australian records in both the 1500m and the Mile events, while in the world of baseball **Jack Doyle**, born in 1869 in Killorglin, Ireland, later became a celebrated first baseman in Major League Baseball after immigrating to America.

Also in baseball **Larry Doyle**, better known as 'Laughing Larry' was a second baseman in Major League Baseball from between 1907 to 1920. Born in 1886 in Caseyville, Illinois, he died in 1974.

Not many Doyles can boast of a postage stamp issued in their honour – but that is certainly the case with the former Irish hurler **John Doyle**, born in 1930 at Holycross, in Co. Tipperary.

A hurler with Tipperary from 1949 to 1967, the Irish postage stamp in his honour was issued in 2000.

Another noted former hurler who played with Tipperary is **Jimmy Doyle**, born in 1939 and who played between 1957 and 1973.

In the sport of lacrosse **Colin 'Popeye' Doyle**, born in 1977 in Kitchener, Ontario is, at the time of writing, a player for the San Jose Stealth of the National Lacrosse League, while in the boxing ring **Jack Doyle** was the Irish boxer, tenor, and actor who was born in 1913 in Cobh.

Known as 'The Gorgeous Gael' he led a fast-paced life of drinking, gambling, and partying.

Shortly before his death in 1978 he had been asked if he had any regrets over the money he had squandered, to which he replied: 'None at all, 'twas never a generous man that went to hell!'

Doyles have also gained distinction on the field of battle.

Born in 1891 in New Ross, Co. Wexford, **Martin Doyle** was an Irish recipient of the Victoria Cross, the highest award for gallantry for British and Commonwealth forces, following an action on the Western Front during the First World War.

He died in 1940.

Also during the terrible carnage of the First World War **Father Willie Doyle**, born in 1873 at Dalkey, was the Irish Jesuit priest and military chaplain who was awarded the Military Cross for his bravery in action.

He was killed in action at Ypres in August of 1917.

Key dates in Ireland's history from the first settlers to the formation of the Irish Republic:

circa 7000 B.C.	Arrival and settlement of Stone Age people.
circa 3000 B.C.	Arrival of settlers of New Stone Age period.
circa 600 B.C.	First arrival of the Celts.
200 A.D.	Establishment of Hill of Tara, Co. Meath, as seat of the High Kings.
circa 432 A.D.	Christian mission of St. Patrick.
800-920 A.D.	Invasion and subsequent settlement of Vikings.
1002 A.D.	Brian Boru recognised as High King.
1014	Brian Boru killed at battle of Clontarf.
1169-1170	Cambro-Norman invasion of the island.
1171	Henry II claims Ireland for the English Crown.
1366	Statutes of Kilkenny ban marriage between native Irish and English.
1529-1536	England's Henry VIII embarks on religious Reformation.
1536	Earl of Kildare rebels against the Crown.
1541	Henry VIII declared King of Ireland.
1558	Accession to English throne of Elizabeth I.
1565	Battle of Affane.
1569-1573	First Desmond Rebellion.
1579-1583	Second Desmond Rebellion.
1594-1603	Nine Years War.
1606	Plantation' of Scottish and English settlers.
1607	Flight of the Earls.
1632-1636	Annals of the Four Masters compiled.
1641	Rebellion over policy of plantation and other grievances.
1649	Beginning of Cromwellian conquest.
1688	Flight into exile in France of Catholic Stuart monarch James II as Protestant Prince William of Orange invited to take throne of England along with his wife, Mary.
1689	William and Mary enthroned as joint monarchs; siege of Derry.
1690	Jacobite forces of James defeated by William at battle of the Boyne (July) and Dublin taken.

1691	Athlone taken by William; Jacobite defeats follow at Aughrim, Galway, and Limerick; conflict ends with Treaty of Limerick (October) and Irish officers allowed to leave for France.
1695	Penal laws introduced to restrict rights of Catholics; banishment of Catholic clergy.
1704	Laws introduced constricting rights of Catholics in landholding and public office.
1728	Franchise removed from Catholics.
1791	Foundation of United Irishmen republican movement.
1796	French invasion force lands in Bantry Bay.
1798	Defeat of Rising in Wexford and death of United Irishmen leaders Wolfe Tone and Lord Edward Fitzgerald.
1800	Act of Union between England and Ireland.
1803	Dublin Rising under Robert Emmet.
1829	Catholics allowed to sit in Parliament.
1845-1849	The Great Hunger: thousands starve to death as potato crop fails and thousands more emigrate.
1856	Phoenix Society founded.
1858	Irish Republican Brotherhood established.
1873	Foundation of Home Rule League.
1893	Foundation of Gaelic League.
1904	Foundation of Irish Reform Association.
1913	Dublin strikes and lockout.
1916	Easter Rising in Dublin and proclamation of an Irish Republic.
1917	Irish Parliament formed after Sinn Fein election victory.
1919-1921	War between Irish Republican Army and British Army.
1922	Irish Free State founded, while six northern counties remain part of United Kingdom as Northern Ireland, or Ulster; civil war up until 1923 between rival republican groups.
1949	Foundation of Irish Republic after all remaining constitutional links with Britain are severed.